MEL BAY PRESENTS

By Jerry Silverman

Contents

HOME

Do They Miss Me At Home? 6

Home, Sweet Home 4

In the Good Old Summertime 36

Long, Long Ago 46

Mr. & Mrs. Brown 30

New Friends, True Friends 28

Old Dog Tray 21

The Old Oaken Bucket 8

Over the Garden Wall 22

Over the Mountain 53

Rocked In the Cradle Of the Deep 33

School Days 10

Some Folks 25

The Songs of the Olden Days 12

The Stranger Man 48

There's Music in the Air 16

What Shall I Offer Thee? 26

Willie, We Have Missed You 44

You'll Miss Lots Of Fun When You're Married . . 18

30-Second Songs

Answer the First Rap 41

Doan' Yo' Lis'n 40

First Ask Yourself 39

A Good Exercise 42

How To Find Success 41

Keep Awake 43

Making the Best Of It 39

Now and Then 43

The Pleasure of Giving 40

A Present From Yourself 42

To Understand 39

When They Say Unkind Things 42

HOME RUNS

Base Ball Fever 62

Hurrah For Our National Game 65

Slide, Kelly, Slide! 55

Take Me Out To the Ball Game 60

Tally One For Me 58

HEARTBREAK

Ben Bolt 86

The Dying Nun 97

From The Land Of The Sky-Blue Water 103

Hard Times, Come Again No More 70

The Horticultural Wife 78

Jockey Hat And Feather 76

Lily Bell 80

Lula Is Gone 72

Nelly Was A Lady 75

On The Road To Mandalay 99

Pilgrim Stranger 88

Rock Me To Sleep, Mother 84

Rosalie, The Prairie Flower 108

Ship On Fire 90

Too Late For Love 110

Twenty Years Ago 82

Under the Willow She's Sleeping 74

The Voices That Are Gone 68

What Care I? 106

Introduction

Long before I ever began working on this book I clipped Russell Baker's article from *The New York Times*. At the time I wasn't sure why I clipped it. It just seemed to sum up the way I felt about making music the old-fashioned way: by actually singing. Anyway, I clipped it and filed it. Then came the book.

As my digging into the dusty vaults of songdom began to yield up half-remembered treasures of bygone days—songs that would have made the hit parades in their times (had the dubious institution existed) —I pulled out the Baker article (I actually remembered where I had stuck it—no mean feat in itself!) and re-read it. It seemed more than ever to strike the right chord and to underscore the very point of this collection: That not only don't they write 'em like they used to, but they don't sing 'em like they used to either.

HEAR AMERICA LISTENING
Russell Baker

My mother used to sing to herself while she ironed. "Redwing" was a favorite, and there was another that must have dated from 1905, 1910, which went, "I wish Mama'd hold her tongue, she had beaus when she was young." Unaware that I was listening, she sang only for herself, sliding the iron back and forth and lost in good memories, I suppose, to which these old tunes transported her, far from the ironing board. Well, everybody used to sing. Not like nowadays. Nowadays we let the technology do the singing for us. It's so nearly perfect, the technology. We couldn't hope to sound a tenth as good if we were bold enough to open the throat and assail in the air.

Nowadays Whitman would not hear America singing. He would hear Japanese technology singing almost perfectly. He would write, "I hear America listening to nearly perfect Japanese technological reproduction of singing."

Why have we become a nation of listeners? Why do we make no music for ourselves anymore? Are we afraid of coming off badly in competition with the superb technology of Japan? Once we used to sing shamelessly around for the pure pleasure of it, and not so long ago either.

We used to sing on long car rides. Lacking the amazingly pure sound of FM car radios, audio cassette machinery and CD players built into the dashboard, we entertained ourselves singing the hits of the day and old-timers from the Bronze Age: "The Isle of Capri," and the one about the old

spinning wheel in the parlor spinning dreams of long, long ago. Jerome Kern, Rodgers and Hammerstein. Songs with tunes.

Well, of course most popular songs nowadays don't have tunes. Tunes are old-hat, tunes are for gummy-eyed Grandpa, tunes are for people so out of it they don't feel the beat or even begin to grasp the complex subtlety of today's popular music, and so forth, all of which is true.

But it is also true that the wonderful songs of today can only be listened to, since it is impossible for 3, or 10, or 30 people to sing a song that has no tune unless they are professional singers. Even professional singers can't always manage it.

Recently two successful singers who go by the improbable name Milli Vanilli lost a prize for great recorded singing when it was discovered that they hadn't done the prize-winning singing. All they'd done was move their lips and pretend to be lost in transports of song while parties unseen were doing the actual singing, just as Cyrano de Bergerac hid in the shadows speaking seductive poetry to Roxanne on behalf of that beautiful dunce, Christian.

What this showed was that modern songs are so hard to sing that even professionals don't always trust themselves to try it. The songs America sang before it started to rock were doubtless simple-minded and certainly not worthy of an age as sophisticated as ours today, but because they were accessible to everybody they contributed to a sense of community that comes from group singing.

Nowadays the nation's only exercise in group singing comes when a sports crowd is urged to stand and join in singing "The Star-Spangled Banner," which is almost as hard to sing as the typical rock 'n' roll chart topper. Everybody stands, of course, but most of the crowd takes the Milli Vanilli way out: lots of lip movement, let the public address system make the sound.

Observing this pathetic weaseling at stadiums and ball parks, I often think of the unbridled pleasure with which massed audiences used to sing in huge movie houses, following the bouncing ball to simple tunes thundered out by an organist spotlighted in the pit.

Americans sang, too, all the way through World War II. The songs may have been silly, melancholy, propagandistic and sentimental, but singing them helped Americans identify a communal identity for themselves. Nowadays the absence of singing defines our lack of communal identity, our national apartness, our aloneness.

It speaks too of our submissive relationship with machines, a relationship in which machines do all the talking and all the singing and we do all the listening. To be sure, the typical rock concert generates an intense sense of community. It is the community of people overpowered by amplifying machinery, which is the destiny of a nation of listeners.

Home, Sweet Home

1829

Henry Bishop (1786—1855) was an English composer of operas, operettas and songs. The song, "Home, Sweet Home" occurs repeatedly in numerous variations and sung by various voices in his 1829 opera of the same name. Edward Rimbault, writing in *Grove's Dictionary*, had this to say about it: "...if 'Home, Sweet Home' is sentimentally beloved beyond its deserts, mainly because it was exploited by so many prima donnas of the 19th century, it still remains a good tune."

Words and Music by
Henry R. Bishop

An exile from home, splendor dazzles in vain,
Oh, give me my lowly thatched cottage again;
The birds singing gaily, that come at my call;
Give me them, with that peace of mind, dearer than all. *Chorus*

To thee, I'll return, overburdened with care,
The heart's dearest solace will smile on me there.
No more from that cottage again will I roam,
Be it ever so humble, there's no place like home. *Chorus*

Do They Miss Me At Home?

Do they miss me at home, Do they miss me? 'Twould be an as- sur- ance most

dear, To know that this mo - ment some loved one_____ Was

say - ing; "I wish he were here." To feel that the group at the

fire - side were think - ing of me as I roam; Oh

yes, 'twould be joy with-out meas-ure,_____ To know that they miss me at home._____ To know that they miss me at home._____

When the twilight approaches the season
That ever is sacred in song,
Does someone repeat my name over,
And sigh that I tarry so long?
And is there a chord in the music
That's missed when my voice is away?
And a chord in each heart that awaketh,
Regret my wearisome stay,
Regret my wearisome stay?

Repeat first verse

7

The Old Oaken Bucket

c. 1820

Words by Samuel Woodworth

Music by George Kiallmark

The moss-covered bucket I hailed as a treasure,
For often at noon when returned from the field,
I found it the source of an exquisite pleasure,
The purest and sweetest that nature can yield.
How ardent I seized it with hands that were glowing.
And quick to the white-pebbled bottom it fell;
The soon, with the emblem of truth overflowing
And dripping with coolness, it rose from the well.
The old oaken bucket, the iron-bound bucket,
The moss-covered bucket that hung in the well.

9

School Days

1907

German immigrant Gus Edwards and his collaborator combined their talents to compose many popular songs in the first decade of the 20th century. "School Days" was their greatest success. It sold over three million copies of sheet music when it was first published in 1907—an amazing figure when one realized that in those days the promotion of a song was literally a "word-of-mouth" undertaking.

Words by Will D. Cobb

Music by Gus Edward

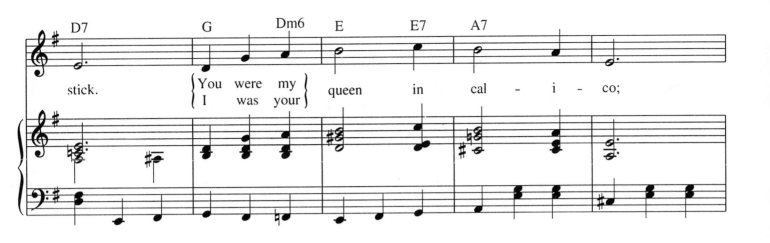

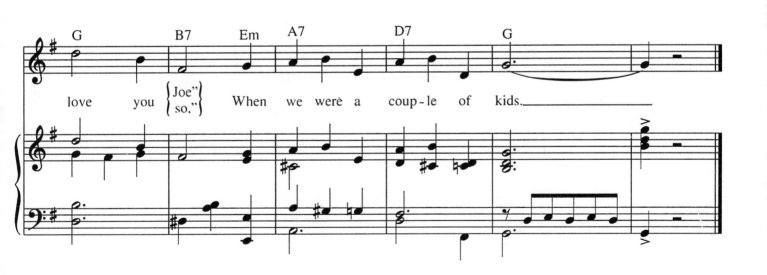

The Songs Of The Olden Days

1872

George Frederick Root (1820—1895) is chiefly remembered today for his stirring and sentimental songs of the Civil War: "The Battle Cry of Freedom," "Just Before the Battle, Mother," and "Tramp, Tramp, Tramp" are among his best known compositions.

Words and Music by
George F. Root

com-ing thro' the rye, my dear, Yes, Com-ing thro' the rye, Our

hearts were fill'd with sweet - est dreams, We were com-ing thro' the rye. A -

las! that those vis - ions could not re - main, They went with the ebb - ing tide, As we

ten - der - ly watch'd in grief _ and _ pain, While the last rose of sum-mer died, While the

last rose of sum - mer died. But the Au - tumn has joys to the spring un-known, And a rest for ___ those that ___ roam; ___ The dear - est ___ treas - ure of all is our own, We have home, home, ___ Sweet, sweet home, There's no ___ place like home, ___ There's no ___ place like home.

15

There's Music In The Air

1854

Words by Fanny Crosby

Music by George F. Root

There's mu-sic in the air,_____ When the in-fant morn is nigh, And

faint its blush is seen_____ on the bright and laugh-ing sky.

Ma-ny a harp's ecs-tat-ic sound thrills us with its joy pro-found,

While we list, En-chant-ed there, To the mu-sic in the air, air.

There's music in the air,
When the noontide's sultry beam
Reflects a golden light
On the distant mountain stream.
When beneath some grateful shade
Sorrow's aching head is laid,
Sweetly to the spirit there
Comes the music in the air.

2

There's music in the air,
When the twilight's gentle sigh
Is lost on evening's breast,
As its pensive beauties die;
Then, oh, then, the loved ones gone
Wake the pure, celestial song;
Angelic voices greet us there,
In the music in the air.

2

You'll Miss Lots Of Fun When You're Married

1890

Before John Phillip Sousa (1854—1932) got to be known as "The March King," by such compositions as "The Stars and Stripes Forever," and other stirring marches, he had played in an orchestra under Offenbach during that composer's tour of the U.S. in 1876—77, and conducted the U.S. Marine Corps band from 1880—1892. It was while he was conductor of this band, but before he created his immortal marches, that he knocked off this little ditty.

Words by Edward M. Taber

Music by John Philip Sousa

Mat-ri-mo - ni - al life is pro - duc - tive of bliss. As an - y sane man will ad - mit._____ And he who don't seek it is sure - ly re - miss, And has nei - ther wis - dom nor wit._____

Now, what could be sweeter and better in life,
Than avoiding its weary turmoil,
And be welcomed at home by your own little wife,
When you've finished your diurnal toil.
Of course, you must give up your bachelor ways,
And the style that you always have carried,
And think with remorse on your old bachelor ways.
    Spoken. (Still,) -
You'll miss lots of fun when you're married.

O why should a man seek to fresco the town,
Or stay out all night and play draw,
When he at his home might sit peacefully down,
And converse with his mother-in-law.
For love and contentment are better by far
Than a conscience by wickedness harried,
And unhappy, therefore, all bachelors are,
Spoken. (Notwithstanding which, however,)-
You'll miss lots of fun when you're married.

Now please do not think for a moment, my friends,
This is a satirical song,
Or that in its sentiments anything tends
To views that are worldly or wrong.
For when you are wed you so happy will be,
You will wish you had not so long tarried,
And then, I suppose, you will villify me,
Spoken. (But, all the same,)-
You'll miss lots of fun when you're married.

Old Dog Tray

Solo or vocal ensemble,
（ Use piano notes for ensemble ）

Words and Music by
Stephen C. Foster

1. The morn of life is past, And ev'-ning come at last, It brings me a dream of a
2. The forms I call'd my own, Have van-ished one by one, The lov'd ones, the dear ones have
3. When thoughts re-call the past, His eyes are on me cast, I know that he feels what my

once__ hap-py day, Of mer-ry forms I've seen, Up-on the vil-lage, green,
all__ pass'd a-way, Their hap-py smiles have flown, Their gen-tle voi-ces gone; I've
break-ing heart would say; Al-tho' he can-not speak, I'll vain-ly vain-ly seek, A

Chorus

Sport-ing with my old dog Tray.
noth-ing left but old dog Tray. Old dog Tray's ev-er faith-ful. Grief can-not drive him a-
bet-ter friend than old dog Tray.

way, He's gen-tle, he is kind; I'll nev-er, nev-er find A bet-ter friend than old dog Tray.

Over The Garden Wall

Oh, my love stood un - der a wal - nut tree, O - ver the gar - den wall._____ She whis - per'd and said she'd be true to me, O - ver the gar - den wall._____ She'd beau - ti - ful eyes, And beau - ti - ful hair, She was not ve - ry tall, So she stood on a chair, And

23

But her father stamped, and her father raved,
  Over the garden wall,
And like an old madman he behaved,
  Over the garden wall.
She made a bouquet of roses red,
But immediately I popped up my head,
He gave me a bucket of water instead,
  Over the garden wall. *Chorus*

One day I jumped down on the other side,
  Over the garden wall,
And she bravely promised to be my bride,
  Over the garden wall,
But she scream'd in a fright, "here's father, quick,
  I have an impression he's bringing a stick,"
But I brought the impression of half a brick,
  Over the garden wall. *Chorus*

But where there's will, there's always a way,
  Over the garden wall,
There's always a night as well as a day,
  Over the garden wall;
We hadn't much money, but weddings are cheap,
  So while the old fellow was snoring asleep,
With a lad and a ladder she managed to creep
  Over the garden wall. *Chorus*

Some Folks

1858

Words and Music by
Stephen C. Foster

What Shall I Offer Thee?

In 1882, the Oliver Ditson Company of Boston published *The Ideal Method For The Guitar*. The book contained "Operatic and Other Popular Airs, Carefully Selected From The Latest Publications, And Arranged With Special Reference To The Instrument, By Sep. Winner." Septimus Winner (1827—1902) was a prolific composer of music books and popular songs, including such perennial favorites as, "Listen To The Mockingbird." Interestingly, many of his compositions were written under the feminine *nom de plume*, "Alice Hawthorne." In an era when many women writers felt they had to adopt masculine literary identities in order to be published and accepted, Winner's choice of pen name is all the more unusual.

Words and Music by
"Alice Hawthorne" (Septimus Winner)

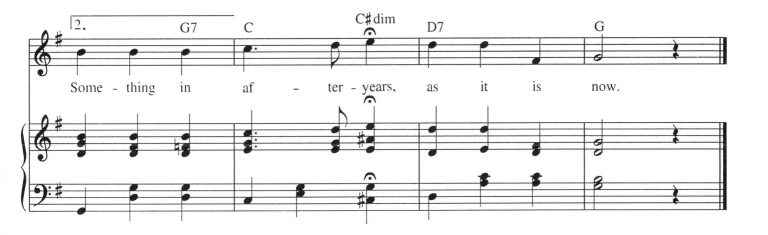

Some - thing in af - ter - years, as it is now.

What shall I offer thee? Life is so strange.
All I can give to thee surely must change!
Give me an ivy leaf, green as the pine,
Give me an ivy leaf, fresh from the vine.)2

What shall I tender thee? Gifts I have none.
What to remember me when I am gone?
Give me an evergreen ere we must part,
Something to hide away close to my heart.)2

New Friends, True Friends

In 1862, Winner wrote a "topical" song entitled, "Give Us Back Our Old Commander: Little Mac, The People's Pride," in honor of Major General George B. McClellan. McClellan had recently been relieved of command of the Army of the Potomac by Lincoln, and Winner's song was judged sufficiently subversive for him to be arrested. He was released from prison after promising to halt the sale of the song. In "New Friends" we find him in a more typically sentimental mood.

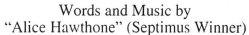

Words and Music by
"Alice Hawthone" (Septimus Winner)

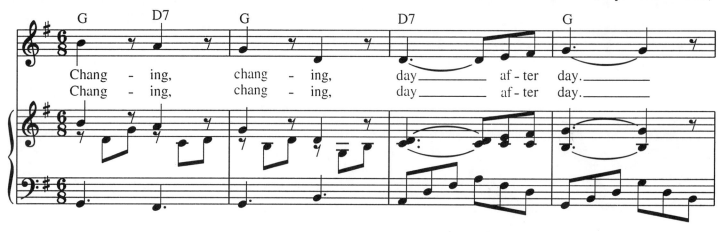

Chang - ing, chang - ing, day_____ af - ter day._____
Chang - ing, chang - ing, day_____ af - ter day._____

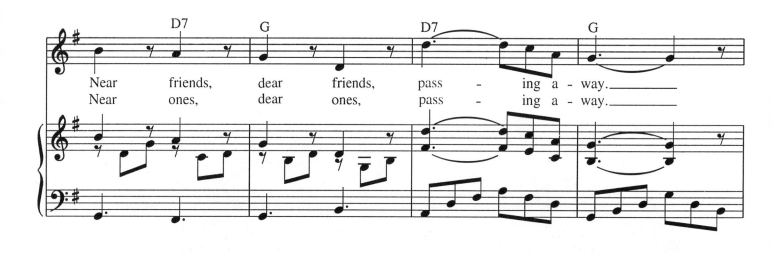

Near friends, dear friends, pass - ing a - way._____
Near ones, dear ones, pass - ing a - way._____

Scenes _____ that are dear_____ to the heart_____ and the eye,_____
Still _____ as the days_____ with their chang - es de - part,_____

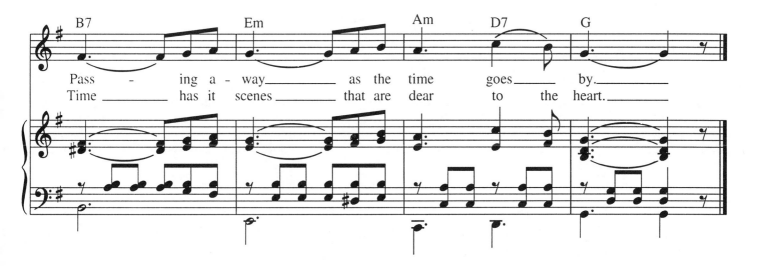

Pass - ing a - way _____ as the time goes _____ by. _____
Time _____ has it scenes _____ that are dear to the heart. _____

D. Maclise, R.A.   T. Landseer.

Mr. & Mrs Brown

Comic Duet
1864

Words by
George Cooper

Music by
Stephen C. Foster

Stephen Collins Foster (1826—1864) often turned to "Negro themes" and "Negro dialect" in his approximately 175 songs. In those *ante bellum* days, his bucolic view of plantation life, (written from his perspective in New York), populated by happy "darkies" who loved "ol' massa," certainly did not conform to reality—to say the least. Nevertheless, quite a number of his songs have endured ("Oh, Susanna," "Camptown Races," "My Old Kentucky Home," among others). In the following four songs we find Foster in his typical comic and sentimental modes.

So Mis-ter Brown, You're come at last, I'm sure it's af-ter two. Dear Mis-tress Brown, Your clock is fast. I know as well as you. O! sir, It's shame-ful, so it is, Don't come, sir, in my sight! Now give me one good kiss to-night, You see that I'm all right, I can-not talk to you to-night, I

Now give me one good kiss to - night, You

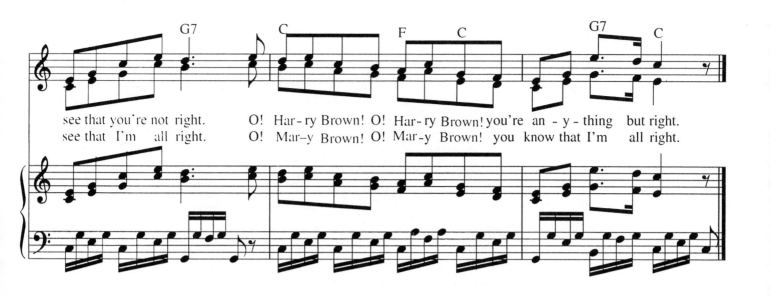

see that you're not right. O! Har-ry Brown! O! Har-ry Brown! you're an-y-thing but right.
see that I'm all right. O! Mar-y Brown! O! Mar-y Brown! you know that I'm all right.

She :	All right! you good for nothing you, Have I not eyes to see?
He :	No, Madam, what I say is true, I'm only on a spree!
She :	Don't make me angry, Mr. Brown, For if you do I'll cry!
He :	I shall not stay to see you frown, So, Mrs. Brown, good bye.

Both :	{ He : I shall not stay to see you frown,
	   So, Mrs. Brown, good bye.
	She : I'll make you stay to see me frown,
	   You shall not say good bye.

Both :	{ He : O! Mary Brown, O! Mary Brown,
	   I'll have to say good bye.
	She : O! Harry Brown, O! Harry Brown,
	   You see you've made me cry.

She (Furiously)

Hard hearted man, I tell you what,
 I must know where you've been;
I am not jealous, O! no! no!
 But it's a shame and sin!
Your bosom friend, young Jones, just left,
 He calls here every night,
I'm sure if it were not for him
 I'd really die with fright.

Both :	{ She : I'm sure if it were not for him,
	   I'd really die with fright.
	He : What Ma'am, if it were not for him
	   You say you'd die with fright!

Both	{ He : Oh! Mary Brown, O! Mary Brown,
	   I'll call him out to fight!
	She : Oh! Harry Brown, O! Harry Brown,
	   He's far above your height.

He (Indignantly)

So, Mr. Jones was here, you say
 While I have been away!
Now Madam you will drive me mad,
 We part this very day.
You know it is my business ma'am
 That keeps me at the store,
And if I could have sooner come (hic)
 I'd been here (hic) long before.

Both :	{ He : You know it is my business ma'am
	   That keeps me at the store.
	She : I know it's not your business, sir
	   That keeps you at the store.

Both :	{ He : O! Mary Brown, O! Mary Brown,
	   It's business at the store.
	She : O! Harry Brown, O! Harry Brown,
	   You've told me that before.

She (Coaxingly)

There, don't be angry, husband, don't!
 I'm sure I love you dear,
I was but joking when I said
 That odious Jones was here.
But promise me, now won't you love,
 That when the night has come
You'll never stay away so late,
 And leave your wife at home.

Both :	{ She : Now promise me when night has come,
	   You'll always stay at home.
	He : I'll promise you when night has come
	   I'll always stay at home.

Both :	{ He : O! Mary Brown, O! Mary Brown,
	   I'll always stay at home.
	She : O! Harry Brown, O! Harry Brown,
	   Now won't you stay at home?

He *(Lovingly)*

You were but joking, dearest wife?
    Now come and kiss me, do,
Jones is a bosom friend to me, *(seriously)*
    But needn't be to you.
My little wife! my joy and life!
    My gentle pretty elf,
If any one sits up with you
    Hereafter, it's myself.

Both: He : If any one sits up with you
            Hereafter, it's myself.
       She : If any one sits up with me,
            O, let it be yourself.

Both: He : O! Mary Brown, O! Mary Brown,
            Our quarrels they are o'er.
       She : O! Harry Brown, O! Harry Brown.
            We'll never quarrel more.

Rocked In The Cradle Of The Deep

1840

English clergyman and composer Joseph Philip Knight (1812—1887) wrote this, his best-known song, while on a visit to the U.S.A. It was introduced and sung here with great success by the English tenor, John Braham, who toured the United States in 1840—42, offering programs of operatic arias, Handelian airs and English ballads.

Words by Hart Willard

Music by
Joseph Phillip King

Rocked in   the cra-dle of the deep,_____   I lay me down_____   in peace to
such   the   trust that still were mine,_____   Tho' storm-y winds_____   swept o'er the

sleep;   Se - cure,   I rest up - on the wave,_____   For thou, O!
brine;   Or tho'   the tem-pest's fier- y breath_____   Rous'd me from

Lord,_____ hast pow'r   to   save.   I   know   Thou wilt not slight my
sleep_____   to wreck   and

call,   For Thou   dost mark the spar-row's fall!   And calm   and peace-ful is my

sleep,_____ Rocked in   the cra-dle of   the deep.   And calm   and peace-ful is my

sleep,_____ Rocked in   the cra-dle of   the deep.   And

death!   In   o -   cean cave still safe with

In The Good Old Summertime

1902

Words by Ren Shields

Music by George Erans

To swim in the pool you'd play "hooky" from school,
Good old summer time.
You'd play "ring arosie" with Jim, Kate and Josie,
Good old summer time.
Those days full of pleasure we now fondly treasure,
When we never thought it a crime
To go stealing cherries, with face brown as berries,
Good old summer time. *Chorus*

30-Second Songs
Making The Best Of It

Carrie Jacobs Bond (1862—1946) had great difficulty finding publishers who would accept her songs. She took matters into her own hands, when after organizing a successful recital of her songs, she founded her own publishing company. Her most widely known song is "I Love You Truly." These "30-Second Songs," (which, individually, take less than thirty seconds to perform) may be likened to "musical fortune cookies."

Words and Music by
Carrie Jacobs Bond

Doan' Yo' Lis'n

No mat - tah w'at dey said, Keep a - walk - in' straight a - haid, W'y, Dey'll

praise yo' when yo' daid. But doan' yo' lis - 'n.

The Pleasure Of Giving

Original Key:E♭

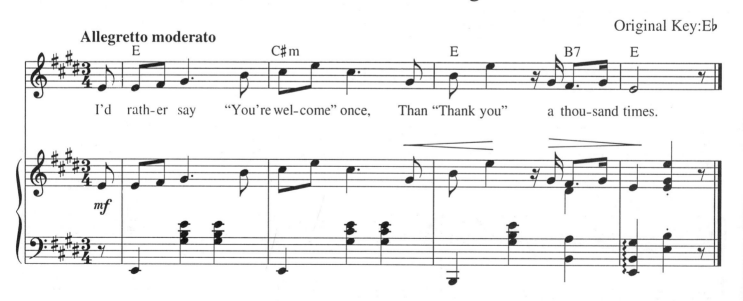

I'd rath-er say "You're wel-come" once, Than "Thank you" a thou-sand times.

How To Find Success

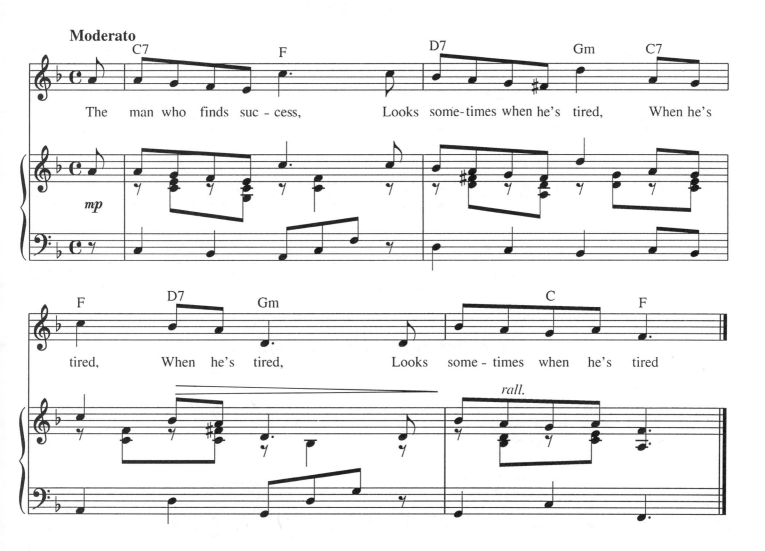

Moderato

The man who finds suc - cess, Looks some-times when he's tired, When he's
tired, When he's tired, Looks some - times when he's tired

Answer The First Rap

Original Key: E♭

Recit.

Op-por- tun-i- ty may knock of -ten, But it's bet-ter to an-swer the first rap!

A Good Exercise

Original Key: E♭

With e-vil things you'll al-ways find It's best to be deaf, dumb and blind.

A Present From Yourself

A friend is a pres-ent you give your-self.

When They Say Unkind Things

Original Key: A♭

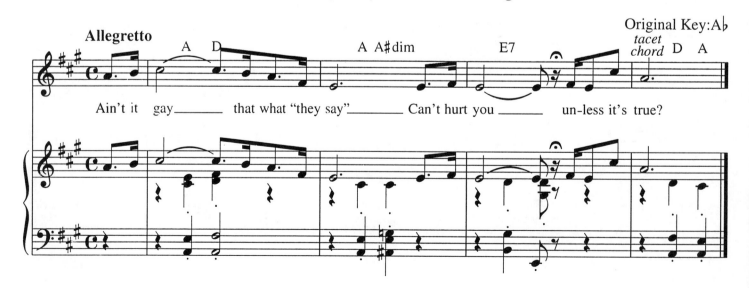

Ain't it gay_____ that what "they say"_____ Can't hurt you _____ un-less it's true?

42

Now And Then

Andante

The "luck-y" fel-low gets up – at five (A.M.); and gen-'ral-ly works till ten (P.M.); But the

oth – er fel-low, Not quite so "luck-y," Works hard ___ just now ___ and then! _____

molto rit.

Keep Awake

Original Key: B♭

Drowsily

Suc-cess nev-er comes to the sleep – ing.

rall.

Willie, We Have Missed You

1854

Words and Music by
Stephen C. Foster

Oh! Wil - lie is it you, dear, Safe, safe at home? They did not tell me time, dear, They said you would not come, I heard you at the gate, And it made my heart re - joice; For I knew that wel - come foot - step, And that dear fa - mil - iar voice, Mak - ing

We've longed to see you nightly,
But this night of all,
The fire was blazing brightly,
And lights were in the hall.
The little ones were up
'Till 'twas ten o'clock and past,
Then their eyes began to twinkle,
And they've gone to sleep at last.
But they listened for your voice
Will they thought you'd never come:
    Oh! Willie, we have missed you,
    Welcome, welcome home!

The days were sad without you,
The nights were long and drear.
My dreams have been about you,
Oh! welcome, Willie dear!
Last night I wept and watch'd
By the moonlight's cheerless ray,
'Till I thought I heard your footstep,
Then I wiped my tears away.
But my heart grew sad again,
When I found you had not come:
    Oh! Willie, we have missed you,
    Welcome, welcome home!

Long, Long Ago

1843

Words and Music by
Thomas H. Bayly

Tell me the tales that to me were so dear, Long, long a-go,

Long, long a-go. Sing me the songs I de-light-ed to hear,

Long, long a-go, long a-go. Now you are come, All my

grief is re-moved, Let me for-get that so long you have roved.

Let me be-lieve that you love as you loved, Long, long a-go, long a-go.

Do you remember the path where we met,
Long, long ago, long, long ago,
Ah, yes, you told me you ne'er would forget,
Long, long ago, long ago.
Then, to all others my smile you preferred,
Love, when you spoke, gave a charm to each word,
Still my heart treasures the praises I heard,
Long, long ago, long ago.

Tho' by your kindness my fond hopes were raised,
Long, long ago, long, long ago,
You by more eloquent lips have been praised,
Long, long ago, long ago.
But, by long absence your truth has been tried,
Still to your accents I listen with pride,
Blessed as I was when I sat by your side,
Long, long ago, long ago.

The Stranger-Man

1902

George Whitefield Chadwick (1854—1931) studied composition in Leipzig in 1878—79. Upon his return to America, he settled in Boston, where he taught harmony, composition and orchestration at the New England Conservatory of Music. He became its director in 1897. His works include operas, choral compositions, symphonies, chamber music and songs.

The piano arrangement of "The Stranger-Man" is Chadwick's original.

Guitarists may place capo on 3rd fret
and play chords in parentheses.

Words by Arthur Macy
Music by George Whitefield Chadwick

gave it un - to me, And it is pass - ing red, be -

cause It was the last of three.

A kiss, in - deed, my daugh - ter dear! I____

mar - vel in sur - prise! Such con - duct with a

stran - ger - man, I fear me, was not wise. Me -

thought the same, my moth - er___ dear, And so at three for -

bore. Al - though the cour - teous stran - ger - man Vowed

he___ had man - y more.

Guitarists may remove capo during interlude to play chords in G or continue playing chords in parentheses.

50

51

stran - ger - man   That hath a kiss to spare.

Over The Mountain

This traditional song appears in the same *Ideal Method For The Guitar* that includes Septimus Winner's songs. It has become a favorite showpiece for five-string banjo players, notably Uncle Dave Macon and Pete Seeger.

A - way and a-way we bound o'er the moun-tain, O - ver the moun-tain, O - ver the moun-tain,

O - ver the val-leys, The hills and the foun-tain, A - way to the chase, a - way, a - way. We

heed not the tem-pest, The wild wind or dan-ger, But joy-ous-ly shout-ing, A- way goes the ran-ger,

Joy - ous-ly shout-ing a - way goes the dan-ger, A- way to the chase, a - way, a - way.

Away and away our wild steeds are bounding,
Wild steeds are bounding, wild steeds are bounding,
Thro' brake and thro' valley our shouts are resounding:
Away to the chase, away, away.
    Oh, list to the hounds' bells, sweetly ringing,
    Over the hills the wild deer is springing,
    Over the hills the wild deer is springing,
    Away to the chase, away, away.

See there the wild deer, trembling, panting,
Trembling, panting - trembling, panting,
Fearfully pausing, one moment standing,
Away to the chase, away, away.
    He's gone boys, he's gone, pursue him, pursue him,
    Hurrah, boys, hurrah! I see him, I see him,
    Hurrah, boys, hurrah! I see him, I see him,
    Away to the death of the wild Ashe Deer.

Slide, Kelly, Slide!

Comic Song
Written & Composed by J. W. Kelly, for
Miss Maggie Cline
1899

I play'd a game of base-ball, I be - long to Ca - sey's Nine! The crowd was feel - ing jol - ly, And the weath-er it was fine. A no - bler lot of play - ers, I think were nev - er found, When the om - ni - bus-es land-ed That day up - on the ground. The game was quick-ly start-ed, They sent me to the bat; I

made two strikes, Says Ca - sey, "What are you strik - ing at?" I

made the third, The catch - er muff'd, And to the ground it fell; Then I

run like a div - il to first-base, When the gang be - gan to yell:

Chorus Slide, Kel - ly,

Slide! your run - ning's a dis - grace! Slide, Kel - ly, slide! Stay

there and hold your base! If some-one does-n't steal ya, And your bat-ting does-n't fail ya, They'll take you to Aus-tra-lia! Slide, Kel-ly, Slide!

'Twas in the second inning,
They called me in, I think,
To take the catcher's place,
While he went to get a drink.
But something was the matter,
Sure I couldn't see the ball;
And the second one that came in
Broke my muzzle, nose and all.
    The crowd up in the grandstand,
    They yelled with all their might,
    I ran towards the Club House,
    I thought there was a fight.
    Twas the most unpleasant feeling,
    I ever felt before;
    I knew they had me rattled,
    When the gang began to roar: *Chorus*

They sent me out to centrefield,
I didn't want to go;
The way my nose was swelling up,
I must have been a show!
They said on me depended,
Our vict'ry or defeat.
If a blind man was to look at us,
He'd know that we were beat.
    "Sixty-four to nothing!"
    Was the score when we got done,
    And ev'rybody there but me,
    Said they had lots of fun.
    The news got home ahead of me,
    They heard I was knock'd out;
    The neighbors carried me in the house,
    And then began to shout: *Chorus*

Tally One For Me

Polka

Words and Music by
John T. Rutledge

I'm the pride and pet of all the girls That come out to the park, My ev-'ry play out in the field, You bet they're sure to mark, And when you see them smil-ing, And their hands go pit-a-pat, Just mark it down, For num-ber one is go-ing to the bat. Oh!

I never knock the ball up high,
Or even make it bound,
But always send it whizzing,
Cutting daisies in the ground.
I always make a clean base hit,
And go around, you see-
And that's the reason why I say,
Just tally one for me. *Chorus*

I soon will stop my "balling,"
For my heart is led astray.
'Twas stolen by a nice young girl.
By her exquisite play.
And after we are maried,
Why, I hope you'll come to see.
The "tally" I have made for life,
And mark it down for me. *Chorus*

Take Me Out To The Ball Game

1908

Words by Jack Norworth

Music by Albert Von Tilzer

Take me out to the ball game,

Take me out with the crowd._____ Buy me some pea-nuts and

Crack - er Jack; I don't care if I nev - er get back. Let me

root, root, root for the home team; If they don't win, it's a

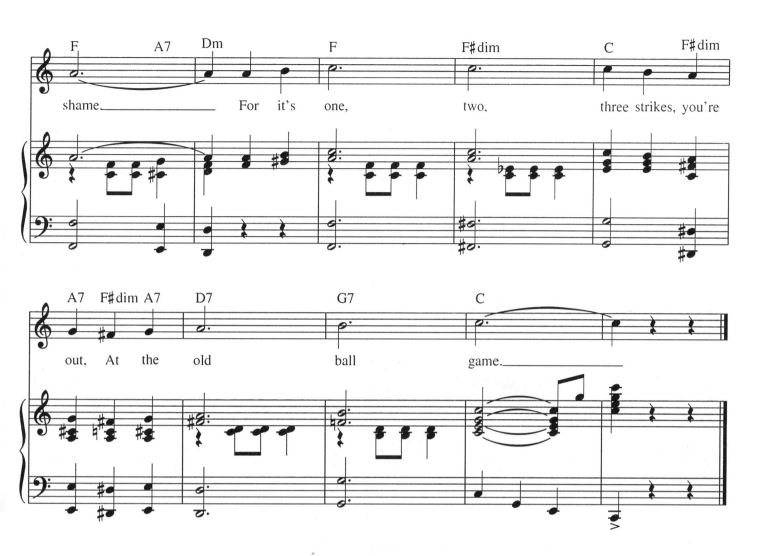

shame._____ For it's one, two, three strikes, you're out, At the old ball game._____

Base Ball Fever

1867

Composer Unknown

63

Our Merchants have to close their stores
    Their clerks away are staying,
Contractors too, can do no work,
    Their hands are all out playing;
There's scarce a day that folks don't run,
    As true as I'm a liver;
To see a match 'bout to be played,
    'Cause they've the Base Ball fever. *Chorus*

To be in fashion, ladies too,
    In place of Waterfalls sirs;
Way back behind the ears, they wear,
    An awful big Base Ball sirs;
I shouldn't wonder but 'ere long,
    Each Miss, if you'll perceive her,
Will carry Bats all through her hair-
    'Cause she too has the fever. *Chorus*

Our little boys as well as big,
    All, to the Bat are taking;
And smarter folks are coining cash,
    At Bat and Base Ball making:
You cannot walk along the street,
    I'll bet my patent lever;
That two boys ain't a-playing catch,
    'Cause they've the Base Ball fever. *Chorus*

Our papers teem with base ball news,
    Four columns good and over;
Our stores now sell more bats and balls
    Than would, three acres cover
We've clubs no end, and players sharp,
    But I will bet my Beaver;
That I can *catch*, as well as they,
    For I have *kotcht* the fever. *Chorus*

Hurrah For Our National Game

1869

The first baseball game played under "modern rules"—as drawn up by Alexander J. Cartwright—took place on June 19, 1846 at the Elysian Fields in Hoboken, New Jersey. The "New Yorkers" beat the "Knickerbockers" 23 to 1 in four innings.

Words and Music by
Walter Neville

Tempo di marcia

Hur-rah for our game, Our Na-tion-al___ Game, There's__ health in its ev-'ry bound. A thrill of de-light in its ve-ry name, A joy in its sim-ple sound. It lends new__ strength to our har-dy__ race, And its pleas-ures__ are nev-er tame.___ Then___

here's to the bat, the ball and the base: Hur-rah for our Na - tion-al

Game._____ Then hur-rah for our Na - tion-al Game, Hur-rah, Here's a

cheer for its well - earned fame. Suc - cess to it ev - er, Hur -

rah, Hur-rah, Hur - rah for our Na - tion-al Game.

The timid lament o'er such dangerous fun,
And groan at "that terrible ball."
The lazy ones shrink from making "a run,"
And cowards are fearing a fall.
  But give us the dash of a strong "home strike,"
  And we laugh such weak folly to shame.
  Take all other sports and do what you like,
  But leave us our National Game.*Chorus*

The Gamester may boast of the pleasures of play,
The Billiardist brag of his cue.
The Horse Jockey gabble of next racing day,
The Yachtsman discourse of the blue.
  The patrons of Racket feast on its joys,
  Whilst Cricket its lovers inflame.
  Croquet's very well for young ladies and boys,
  But give us the National Game. *Chorus*

Now toss for the innings, the bases are down,
Outsiders go into the field.
The scorer with tallies successes will crown,
As each striker "the willow" doth wield.
  The Captains assign each player his place,
  The Umpire his rulings will name.
  To all their decisions submit with good grace,
  As required by our National Game. *Chorus*

And thus 'tis in life, each one has a post,
Assigned by the Captain of all.
While great Umpire "Conscience" is guiding the host,
Take heed that we list to his call.
  May no "base play" be ours, may our record be bright,
  With no "foul deeds" our "clean score" to shame.
  Let us play life's game nobly, respecting the right,
  As we do in our National Game. *Chorus*

The Voices That Are Gone

Words and Music by
Stephen C. Foster

Sweet as wood dove's note when calling
To her mate as night draws on,
Soft as snowflakes lightly falling,
Come the voices that are gone.
        Voices heard in days of childhood,
        Softly at the hour of prayer.
        Or loud ringing through the wildwood,
        When the young heart knew no care. *Chorus*

So when life's bright sun is setting,
And its day is well-nigh done,
May there be no vain regretting
Over mem'ries I would shun.
        But when death is o'er, to meet me,
        May such much-loved forms come on,
        And the first sounds that shall greet me
        Be the voices that are gone. *Chorus*

Hard Times, Come Again No More

Words and Music by
Stephen C. Foster

days you have lin-gered a - round my cab - in door, Oh! Hard Times, come a - gain no more.

While we seek mirth and beauty,
And music light and gay,
There are frail forms fainting at the door.
Though their voices are silent,
Their pleading looks will say,
Oh! Hard Times, come again no more. *Chorus*

There's a pale drooping maiden
Who toils her life away,
With a worn heart whose better days are o'er.
Though her voice would be merry,
'Tis sighing all the day,
Oh! Hard Times, come again no more. *Chorus*

'Tis a sigh that is wafted
Across the troubled wave,
'Tis a wail that is heard upon the shore.
'Tis a dirge that is murmured
Around the lowly grave,
Oh! Hard Times, come again no more. *Chorus*

Lula Is Gone

1858

Words and Music by
Stephen C. Foster

1. With a heart for-sak - en I wan - der, In si - lence, in grief and a-
2. Not a voice a-wak - ens the mount - ains, No glad - ness re-turns with the
3. When I view the chill - blight- ed bow - ers, And roam o'er the snow cov-ered

lone, On a form de-part - ed I pon - der, For
dawn, Not a smile is mir-rored in the fount - ains, For
plain, How I long for spring's bud-ding flow - ers, To

Lu - la, sweet Lu - la is gone. Gone when the ro - ses have fad - ed,
Lu - la, sweet Lu - la is gone. Day is be -reft of its pleas - ures,
wel - come her sweet smiles a - gain. Why does the earth seem for - sak - en?

Gone when the mead - ows are bare,
Night of its beau - ti - ful dream,
Time will this sad - ness re - move,

To a land by or – ange blos- soms
While the dirge of well re - mem-bered
At her voice the mead ows will a -

shad - ed, Where sum- mer ev - er lin - gers on the air.
meas - ures, Is mur-mured by the rip - ples on the stream.
wak - en, To ver - dure, sweet mel - o - dy and love.

Chorus (very slowly)

Lu - la, Lu - la, Lu - la is gone, With summer birds her bright smiles, To sun-ny lands have flown. When

day break-eth glad - ly, My heart wak-eth sad - ly, For Lu - la, - Lu la is gone

Under The Willow She's Sleeping

1860

Words and Music by
Stephen C. Foster

1. Un - der the wil - low she's laid with care, (Sang a lone moth - er while weep - ing,)
2. Un - der the wil - low no songs are heard, Near where my darl - ing lies dream - ing,
3. Un - der the wil - low by night and day, Sor - row - ing ev - er I pon - der;
4. Un - der the wil - low I breathe a prayr, Long - ing to lin - ger for - ev - er,

Un - der the wil - low, with gold - en hair, My lit - tle one's qui - et - ly sleep - ing.
Nought but the voice of some far - off bird, Where life and its plea - sures are beam - ing.
Free from its shad - ow - y gloom - y ray; Ah! nev - er a - gain can she wan - der.
Near to my an - gel with gold - en hair, In lands where there's sor - row - ing nev - er.

Chorus

Fair, fair and gold - en hair, (Sang a lone moth - er while weep - ing.) Un - der the wil - low she's sleep - ing.

Nelly Was A Lady
1845

Words and Music by
Stephen C. Foster

Down on the Mis-sis-sip-pi float - ing, Long time I trav-el on the way.

All night the cot-ton-wood a - tot - ing, Sing for my true love all the day.

Chorus

Nel-ly was a la-dy, Last night she died; Toll the bell for love-ly Nell, My dark Vir - gin - ia bride.

Now I'm unhappy and I'm weeping,
Can't tote the cottonwood no more.
Last night while Nelly was a-sleeping,
Death came a-knocking at the door. *Chorus*

When I saw Nelly in the morning,
Smile till she opened up her eyes.
Seemed like the light of day a-dawning,
Just 'fore the sun begin to rise. *Chorus*

75

Jockey Hat And Feather

c. 1850

Words by
Fred Wilson

Music by
W. H. Brockway

As I was walk-ing out one day, Think-ing of the weath-er, I saw a pair of rog - uish eyes 'Neath a hat and feath-er; She looked at me, I looked at her, It made my heart pit pat. Then turn - ing 'round she said to me, "How do you like my hat?"

She wore a handsome broadcloth basque
Cut in the latest fashion,
And flowers all around her dress
Made her look quite dashing,
    Her high-heeled boots as she walk'd on
    The pavement, went pit pat.
    I'll ne'er forget the smile I saw
    Beneath that jockey hat. *Chorus*

She kissed her hand, said "au revoir,"
Then I was a goner.
Before I'd time to say "good-bye,"
She was 'round the corner.
    I tried that night, but could not sleep,
    So up in bed I sat,
    And right before my face I thought
    I saw that jockey hat. *Chorus*

The Horticultural Wife

"Written By A Celebrated English Gardener After Disappointment In Love"

1857

The Hutchinson Family was an extremely popular family singing group in the years before and during the Civil War. They were known for their militant Abolitionist and Temperance songs. This unusual song, with its often obscure references to various flowers and plants, is atypical of their repertoire.

Words and Music by
The Hutchinson Family

She's my myr-tle, my ge-ra-ni-um, My sun-flow'r, my sweet mar-jo-ram, My hon-ey-suck-le, my tu-lip, my vi-o-let, My hol-ly-hock, my dahl-ia, my _ mig-non-ette. Ho, ho! she's a

fick-le wild rose, A dam-ask, a cab-bage, a chi - na - rose. Ho, ho! she's a

For Repeats / *Final Ending*

fick-le wild rose, A dam-ask, a cab-bage, That ev-'ry-bod-y knows. She's my ev-'ry-bod-y knows.

She's my snowdrop, my ranunculus,
My hyacinth, my gilly flow'r, my polyanthus,
My heart's ease, my pink, my water lily,
My buttercup, my daisy, my daffy-down-dilly, *Chorus*

I am like a scarlet runner that has lost its stick,
Or a cherry that is left for the dickey birds to pick.
Like a wat'ring pot I'll weep, like a pavion I'll sigh,
Like a mushroom I'll wither, like a cumber I'll die. *Chorus*

I am like a bumblebee that don't know where to settle,
And she is a dandelion and a stinging nettle.
My heart's like a beet-root, choked with chickweed,
My head's like a pumpkin, running off to seed. *Chorus*

I've a mind to make myself a felodese,
And finish of my woes on the branch of a tree.
But I won't, for I know that a my kicking you'll roar,
And in honor of my death with a double encore! *Chorus*

HORTICULTURAL GLOSSARY

mignonette : *Reseda odorata,* small fragrant greenish-white flower
ranunculus : buttercup
polyanthus : hybrid primrose
heartsease : pansy
daffydowndilly : daffodil
damask : variety of rose
cabbage (rose) : *Rosa centrifolia,* upright rose
pavion : poppy (?)

felodese (fel-o-de-say): suicide

Lily Bell
1853

Words by
W. W. Wakelam

Music by
Charles Mueller

O Lil - ly Bell, I'm weep - ing, I'm weep-ing, love, for thee, But thou in death are sleep - ing, Be - neath the wil - low tree, The lit - tle birds are sing - ing, Their songs with mu - sic's swell, But yet my heart is pin - ing for thee, My Lil - ly Bell.

Chorus

O, Lil - ly Bell, I'm weep - ing, I'm weep - ing, Love, for thee, But

thou in death are sleep - ing, Be - neath the wil - low tree.

O Lilly Bell, I'm thinking,
As through the fields I roam,
Of tears we shed at parting,
In that once happy home.
    I'm list'ning for those songs, love,
    This lonely heart to cheer,
    The songs you sang in childhood,
    That angels love to hear. *Chorus*

The summer flow'rs are blooming
Around the farmhouse door,
The little boat is moored, love,
Down by the pebbly shore.
    But, o, my thoughts are weary,
    When other hearts are gay.
    This world to me seems dreary,
    My Lily's far away. *Chorus*

Twenty Years Ago

1856

Words and Music by
William Willing

I've wan-dered to the vil-lage, Tom, I've sat be-neath the tree; Up-on the school-house play-ing ground, Which shel-ter'd you and me. But none were there to greet me, Tom, And few were left to know, That play'd with us up-on the grass, Some twen-ty years a-go.

The grass is just as green, dear Tom, barefooted boys at play
Were sporting just as we did then, with spirits just as gay;
But the Master sleeps upon the hill, which, coated o'er with snow,
Afforded us a sliding place just twenty years ago.

The river's running just as still; the willows on its side
Are larger than they were, dear Tom, the stream appears less wide;
The grapevine swing is ruined now, where once we played the beau,
And swung our sweethearts, "pretty girls," just twenty years ago.

The spring that bubbled neath the hill; close by the spreading beech
Is very low; 'twas once so high that we could almost reach.
And kneeling down to get a drink, dear Tom, I started so,
To see how much that I was changed since twenty years ago.

Near by the spring, upon an elm, you know I cut your name,
Your sweetheart's just beneath it, Tom, and you did mine the same;
Some heartless wretch had peeled the bark, 'twas dying sure but slow,
Just as that one, whose name was cut, died twenty years ago.

My lids have long been dry, dear Tom, but tears came in my eyes.
I thought of her I loved so well, those early-broken ties;
I visited the old churchyard, and took some flowers to strew
Upon the graves of those we loved, some twenty years ago.

Some now are in the churchyard laid, some sleep beneath the sea,
But few are left of our old class, excepting you and me;
And when our time shall come, dear Tom, and we are called to go,
I hope they'll lay us where we played just twenty years ago.

Rock Me To Sleep, Mother

1858

Words by
Elizabeth Akers ("Florence Percy")

Music by John H. Hewitt

O - ver my slum - bers your lov-ing watch keep, Rock me to sleep, Moth-er, Rock me to sleep.

Over my heart in the days that are flown,
No love like mother love ever has shone.
No other worship abides and endures,
Faithful, unselfish and patient like yours.
None like a mother can charm away pain,
From the sick soul and the world-weary brain.
Slumber's soft calms o'er my heavy lids creep,
    Rock me to sleep, mother, rock me to sleep.

Mother, dear mother, the years have been long
Since I last hush'd to your lullaby song.
Sing, then, and unto my soul it shall seem
Womanhood's * tears have been but a dream.
Clasp'd to your heart in a loving embrace,
With your light lashes just sweeping my face.
Never hereafter to wake or to weep,
    Rock me to sleep, mother, rock me to sleep,

* Or, if you prefer : "My manhood's tears..."

Ben Bolt

Words: Unknown

Music by Nelson Kneass

Oh! don't you re-mem-ber sweet Al - ice, Ben Bolt, Sweet Al - ice with hair____ so brown? She wept with de-light when you gave her your smile, And trem-bled with fear____ at your frown. In the old church yard in the val-ley, Ben Bolt, In a corn-er ob-scure and a-

Oh! don't you remember the wood, Ben Bolt,
    Near the green sunny slope of the hill;
Where oft we have sung 'neath its wide-spreading shade,
    And kept time to the click of the mill.
The mill has gone to decay, Ben Bolt,
    And a quiet now reigns all around,
See the old rustic porch, with its roses sweet,
    Lies scatter'd and fallen to the ground.
See the old rustic porch, with its roses so sweet,
    Lies scatter'd and fallen to the ground.

Oh! don't you remember the school, Ben Bolt,
    And the Master so kind and so true,
And the little nook by the clear-running brook,
    Where we gather'd the flow'rs as they grew.
On the master's grave grows the grass, Ben Bolt,
    And the running little brook is now dry;
And of all the friends who were schoolmates then,
    There remains, Ben, but you and I.
And of all the friends who were schoolmates then,
    There remains, Ben, but you and I.

Pilgrim Stranger

c. 1848

4-part choral arrangement

I'm a pil - grim, and I'm a stran - ger, I can tar - ry, I can tar - ry but a night! Do not de - tain me for I am go - ing - To where the foun - tains are ev - er flow - ing; I'm a pil - grim, and I'm a stran - ger, I can tar - ry, I can tar - ry but a night.

There the glory is ever shining;
Oh, my longing heart, my longing heart is there!
Here in this country, so dark and dreary,
I long have wandered forlorn and weary!
 I'm a pilgrim, and I'm a stranger,
 I can tarry, I can tarry but a night.

There's the city to which I journey;
My Redeemer, my Redeemer is its light!
There is no sorrow, nor any sighing,
Nor any tears there, nor any dying!
 I'm a pilgrim, and I'm a stranger,
 I can tarry, I can tarry but a night.

Farewell, neighbors, with tears I've warned you,
I must leave you, I must leave you and be gone!
With this your portion, your heart's desire,
Why will you perish in raging fire!
 I'm a pilgrim, and I'm a stranger,
 I can tarry, I can tarry but a night.

Father, mother and sister, brother!
If you will not journey with me I must go!
Now since your vain hopes you will thus cherish,
Should I too linger and with you perish?
 I'm a pilgrim, and I'm a stranger,
 I can tarry, I can tarry but a night.

Farewell, dreary earth, by sin so blighted,
In immortal beauty soon you'll be arrayed!
He who has formed thee, will soon restore thee,
And then thy dread curse shall never more be:
 I'm a pilgrim, and I'm a stranger,
 Till thy rest shall end the weary pilgrim's night!

Ship On Fire

Henry Russell (1812—1900) was an English composer who studied with Rossini in Naples in 1825, went to Canada about 1833 and was organist of the Presbyterian Church in Rochester, New York, and travelled in America until 1841. When he returned to England he began to give "entertainments" by himself and in company with Charles Mackay (who wrote the text for this song). Some of Russell's well-known songs include, "A Life On The Ocean Wave," and "Woodman, Spare That Tree."
The piano arrangement is Russell's original, complete with all the 19th-century pyrotechnics, reminiscent of his *Maestro*, Rossini.

Guitarists may place capo on 3rd fret and play chords in parentheses.
Diminished chords remain the same.

Words by Charles Mackay
Music by Henry Russell

95

The Dying Nun

Words and Music by
Louis Brewster

Hold my hand so cold and frozen,
Once it was so soft and white.
And this ring that falls down from it,
Clasp'd my finger once so tight.
Little ring they thought so worthless,
That they let me keep it there;
Only a plain golden circlet,
With a braid of Douglass' hair.

Oh, my father, Oh, my mother,
Will you not forgive the past,
When you hear a stranger tell you,
How your stray lamb died at last.
I am coming Douglass, Douglass,
Where you are, I too am there;
Freed at last, I come my dearest,
Death gives back your little Claire.

On The Road To Mandalay
1908

Oley Speaks (1874—1948), American composer and singer, set Rudyard Kipling's famous poem to music in 1908. It was first published in Cincinnati. Speaks himself had great success singing his own composition, and over the years it has become a favorite with hearty baritones on both sides of the Atlantic.

Words by Rudyard Kipling

Music by Oley Speaks

101

'Er petticoat was yaller an' 'er little cap was green,
An' 'er name was Supi-yaw-lat, jes' the same as Theebaw's queen,
An' I seed her first a-smokin' of a whackin' white cheroot,
An' a-wastin' Christian kisses on a 'eathen idol's foot,
    On a 'eathen idol's foot.
Bloomin' idol made of mud,
What they called the Great Gawd Budd,
Plucky lot she cared for idols when I kissed 'er where she stood. *Chorus*

Ship me somewheres east of Suez, where the best is like the worst,
Where there ain't no Ten Commandments, an' a man can raise a thirst.
For the temple bells are callin' and it's there that I would be,
By the old Moulmein pagoda lookin' lazy at the sea,
    Lookin' lazy at the sea.
Come you back to Mandalay,
Where the old Flotilla lay,
Can't you 'ear the paddles chunkin' from Rangoon to Mandalay? *Chorus*

From The Land Of The Sky-Blue Water

1909

American composer Charles Wakefield Cadman (1881—1946) was very interested in American Indian music. He visited the Omaha Indian Reservation, recorded the music he heard there and lectured on it and on Indian customs. In 1909 he published a set of "Four American – Indian songs." "From The Land Of The Sky Blue Water," one of those songs, was made very popular by the opera singer, Lillian Nordica. In 1918 and 1919 his "Indian" opera "Shanweis" ("The Robin Woman") was produced at the Metropolitan Opera in New York.

Words by
Nelle Richmond Eberhart

Music by
Charles Wakefield Cadman

And her eyes they are lit with light-nings,

Her heart is not a - fraid!

But I steal to her lodge at dawn-ing,

What Care I?

Words and Music by
"Alice Hawthorne" (Septimus Winner)

Time is fly-ing, our hopes de-ny-ing, Some are sigh-ing that friends should die __ I've not an-y a-mong the man-y; Why should I. ___ then, why __ should I? Life's a bless-ing not worth __ pos-sess-ing, Friends are few whose hearts __ are true. Our be-gin-ning was full ___ of sin-ning.

106

Vows are spoken, though early broken,
Life's best token soon passes by.
Friends are scattered, and hearts are shattered,
Vainly sighing, but why should I?
    Love, they tell us, is blind and jealous,
    Hearts for gold are bought and sold.
    Man's a creature of fickle feature,
    Woman too, if truth be told. *Chorus*

Doubts awaken, and faith is shaken,
Hearts forsaken that love too well.
All the pleasure we learn to treasure
Brings a sigh to break its spell.
    Truth confided to hearts divided,
    Wakens care we fear to bear.
    Who would borrow from life her sorrow?
    Love is lost - beware, beware! *Chorus*

Rosalie, The Prarie Flower

C.1850

Words and Music by
George F. Root

On the dis – tant prai – rie, Where the heath – er wild,
In that peace – ful dwell – ing was a love – ly child,

In its qui – et beau – ty liv'd and smiled,_____
With her blue eyes beam – ing soft and mild._____

Stands a lit – tle cot – tage, and a creep – ing vine
And the wav – y ring – lets of her flax – en hair,

Loves a – round its porch to twine._____
Float – ing in the sum – mer air,_____

On that distant prairie, when the days were long,
Tripping like a fairy, sweet her song,
With the sunny blossoms, and the birds at play,
Beautiful and bright as they.
When the twilight shadows gather'd in the west,
And the voice of Nature sank to rest,
Like a cherub kneeling, seem'd the lovely child,
With her gentle eyes so mild.
    Fair as a lily, joyous and free,
    Light of that prairie home was she.
    Ev'ry one who knew her felt the gentle pow'r
    Of Rosalie, "The Prairie Flow'r."

But the summer faded, and a chilly blast,
O'er that happy cottage swept at last:
When the autumn song birds woke the dewy morn,
Little "Prairie Flow'r" was gone.
For the angels whisper'd softly in her ear,
"Child, thy Father calls thee, stay not here".
And they gently bore her, rob'd in spotless white,
To their blissful home of light.
    Though we shall never look on her more,
    Gone with the love and joy she bore,
    Far away she's blooming in a fadeless bow'r,
    Sweet Rosalie, "The Prairie Flow'r".

Too Late For Love

1880

Words by Mrs. C. L. Shacklock

Music by T. Frank Allen

She was young and pass-ing fair, Pure and bright, With her wealth of gold-en hair, Eyes of light. And her light-est word and tune were to me like mu-sic's own; She was queen, my heart her throne, Day and night. I can scarce-ly now di-vine why her hand should trem-ble so, As I held it close in mine__ Long a - go. Ah! I

We were standing hand in hand
On the shore,
As again I hope to stand
Nevermore.
Tears had dimm'd her starry eyes,
And her voice was filled with sighs,
Murm'ring words and low replies
O'er and o'er.
    Would I ne'er had left her side,
    Heard the sweet, the last farewell
    Of my gentle promised bride,
    Isabel.
    When she vowed, my wand'rings o'er,
    We should meet to part no more,
    Sadder was the sound it bore,
    Than a knell. *Chorus*

Years had pass'd, I stood again
On the shore,
Finding hope and promise vain
Nevermore.
Shall I meet the glad surprise,
See the love light in her eyes,
Making life a Paradise,
As of yore.
    She is now another's bride:
    All too late I crossed the sea;
    All too late I sought her side,
    Can it be
    That the flowing bridal veil
    Made my darling's cheek so pale?
    Ah! that low and mournful wail
    Answers me. *Chorus*